HANDS-ON HISTORY PROJECTS
INVENTIONS

CONTENTS

SHAPING OUR WORLD

MANY things you do, from reading this book to flying abroad on holiday, would be impossible without the work of inventors. Without Johannes Gutenberg who, in the mid-1400s invented the first printing press in Europe, this book could not have been printed. In 1903, the brothers Orville and Wilbur Wright were the first people to build and fly an aeroplane successfully. The aeroplane that takes you on holiday could not have been built without their pioneering work.

Human beings have been inventing things for thousands of years. The wooden wheel was first used as a means of transport 5,500 years ago. Inventors have also improved upon existing inventions, to shape the world we live in today. Nowadays trains and cars travel on wheels made of metal and rubber at speeds of up to about 200kph. This book is about how inventions have formed today's world.

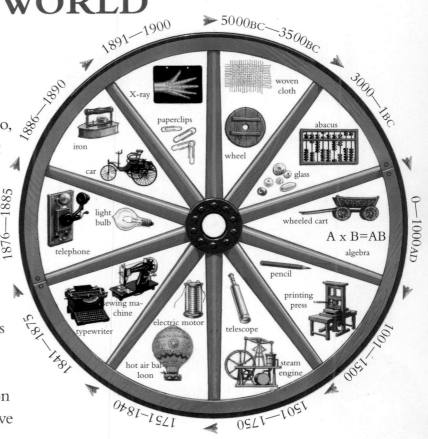

Moving on

In this wheel are some of the objects invented from 4000BC to AD1900 that have fundamentally changed our lives. Follow the arrowheads to see the progression of invention through the ages.

Clean and dry

In the past, people washed clothes by putting them in a tub of hot water and rubbing them with soap. William Sillars invented the first machine for washing clothes in 1890. By turning the big wheel on the lid of the tub, a person could turn the long pegs on the underside of the lid. The moving pegs swirled the clothes around in the tub and so washed out the dirt. The first electric washing machine that washes and spins in a tub, was invented in 1901 by Alva J. Fisher.

modern washing machine

1890 washing machine

HANDS-ON HISTORY PROJECTS
INVENTIONS

DISCOVER SOME OF THE AMAZING TECHNOLOGY OF THE PAST, WITH MORE THAN 20 FUN AND FASCINATING PROJECTS

RACHEL HALSTEAD AND STRUAN REID

southwater

This edition is published by Southwater, an imprint of
Anness Publishing Ltd, Hermes House, 88–89 Blackfriars Road,
London SE1 8HA; tel. 020 7401 2077; fax 020 7633 9499

www.southwaterbooks.com; www.annesspublishing.com

If you like the images in this book and would like to investigate
using them for publishing, promotions or advertising, please visit
our website www.practicalpictures.com for more information.

UK agent: The Manning Partnership Ltd; tel. 01225 478444;
fax 01225 478440; sales@manning-partnership.co.uk
UK distributor: Grantham Book Services Ltd; tel. 01476 541080;
fax 01476 541061; orders@gbs.tbs-ltd.co.uk
North American agent/distributor: National Book Network;
tel. 301 459 3366; fax 301 429 5746; www.nbnbooks.com
Australian agent/distributor: Pan Macmillan Australia;
tel. 1300 135 113; fax 1300 135 103;
customer.service@macmillan.com.au
New Zealand agent/distributor: David Bateman Ltd;
tel. (09) 415 7664; fax (09) 415 8892

ETHICAL TRADING POLICY
Because of our ongoing ecological investment programme, you,
as our customer, can have the pleasure and reassurance of
knowing that a tree is being cultivated on your behalf to naturally
replace the materials used to make the book you are holding.
For further information about this scheme, go to
www.annesspublishing.com/trees

A CIP catalogue record for this book is available from the
British Library.

Publisher: Joanna Lorenz
Managing Editor: Linda Fraser
Editors: Leon Gray, Sarah Uttridge
Designer: Sandra Marques/Axis Design Editions Ltd
Photographers: Paul Bricknell and John Freeman
Illustrators: Rob Ashby, Julian Baker, Andy Beckett, Mark Beesley,
Mark Bergin, Richard Berridge, Peter Bull Art Studio, Vanessa
Card, Stuart Carter, Rob Chapman, James Field, Wayne Ford,
Chris Forsey, Mike Foster, Terry Gabbey, Roger Gorringe, Jeremy
Gower, Peter Gregory, Stephen Gyapay, Ron Hayward, Gary
Hincks, Sally Holmes, Richard Hook, Rob Jakeway, John James,
Kuo Chen Kang, Aziz Khan, Stuart Lafford, Ch'en Ling, Steve
Lings, Kevin Maddison, Janos Marffy, Shane Marsh, Rob McCaig,
Chris Odgers, Alex Pang, Helen Parsley, Terry Riley, Andrew
Robinson, Chris Rothero, Eric Rowe, Martin Sanders, Peter Sarson,
Mike Saunders, Rob Sheffield, Guy Smith, Don Simpson, Donato
Spedaliere, Nick Spender, Clive Spong, Stuart Squires, Roger
Stewart, Sue Stitt, Ken Stott, Steve Sweet, Mike Taylor, Alisa Tingley,
Catherine Ward, Shane Watson, Ross Watton, Alison Winfield,
John Whetton, Mike White, Stuart Wilkinson, John Woodcock
Stylists: Jane Coney, Konika Shakar, Thomasina Smith,
Melanie Williams

Previously published as *Hands-On History: Technology*

Picture credit: The Art Archive:/Oriental Art Museum
Genoa/Dagli Orti, 23tr

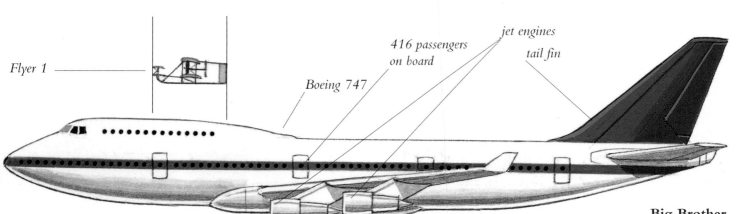

Flyer 1

Boeing 747

416 passengers on board

jet engines

tail fin

Big Brother

The Wright Brothers' first aeroplane, *Flyer 1*, was only 6.4m long. A modern *Boeing 747* is over 10 times bigger, and is almost 71m long. Only one person could fly on *Flyer 1*, while a *Boeing 747-400* can carry 416 passengers. Most modern passenger aircraft, such as the *Boeing*, are powered by jet engines. The jet engine was invented by Sir Frank Whittle in 1930.

It's good to talk

People can make telephone calls from wherever they want using a modern cellular phone such as the one seen here (*right*). The first telephone was invented by Alexander Graham Bell in 1876. He is seen in this engraving. He is testing the first telephone line to run between New York and Chicago, United States, in 1892. Bell's telephone sent voice messages along wires. To make a call, the user's phone had to be connected to a telephone wire. Cellular phones use radio waves and do not need wires.

MAKING LIFE EASIER

WITHOUT the development of bricks and mortar, it would not be possible to build the houses we live in today. People in modern houses, schools, offices and factories can turn on lights and heaters at the flick of a switch, turn taps for water, and look out through windows. In the 1700s and before, people had to fetch water from wells. Today water comes into buildings in pipes under the ground. Before there were electric lights, people used to light candles or lamps burning olive or whale oil.

The wires and pipes that supply electricity, water and gas to buildings today were invented in the 1800s. Many different people took part in their invention. The first electric power station was built in New York in 1884, based on the ideas of Thomas Edison. In the early 1800s, William Murdock, a British inventor, was the first person to set up a factory that produced gas for lighting streets and buildings. In the 1800s too, many people in cities were affected by diseases, such as cholera, that were caused by poor hygiene. Sewer pipes were built to carry drain water away from cities to treatment plants.

Straight and narrow
People used bricks to build gateways such as this 5,000 years ago in the part of the Middle East now called Iraq. These bricks made strong walls that could stand for many years.

Built to last
Gates in the German city of Trier (Trèves) were built almost 2,000 years ago. The mortar (cement) that holds the stones in the gates together was invented by the Romans, who then ruled all of France and parts of Germany. The long-lasting strength of mortar is an important reason why so many ancient Roman buildings have survived to this day.

Onwards and upwards
People are lifting blocks of stone on a winch, standing on scaffolding and cutting stone at the top of the tower in this illustration from the 1400s. Winches and scaffolding made it easier to lift heavy weights and keep stone in place.

Dangerous metal

Lead was used for centuries to make the pipes through which water flowed from reservoirs to houses and public buildings such as baths. Lead dissolves in water and harms the health of the people who drink it. Since the 1950s, plastic water pipes have been used as a safer alternative.

Letting in light

Roman glass tiles, such as this one, were made 2,000 years ago. Ways to make sheets of clear glass for windows were not found until the 1200s. In the 1800s, the British scientist, Michael Faraday, invented ways of making really large panes of glass.

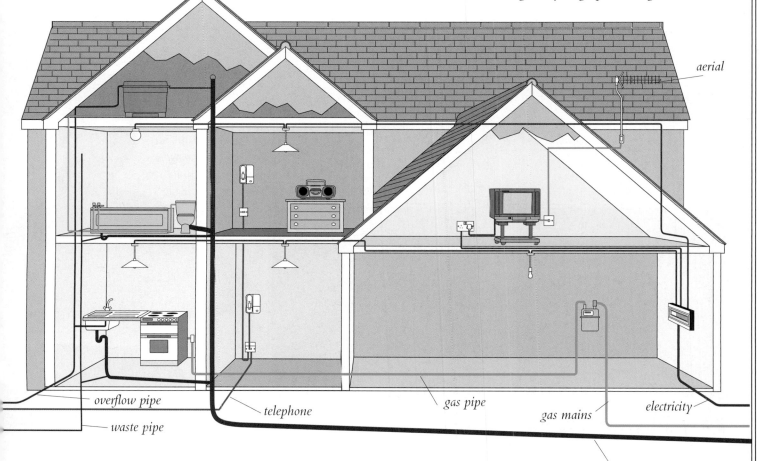

aerial

overflow pipe

telephone

gas pipe

gas mains

electricity

waste pipe

water mains

The modern home

A cross-section of a modern house shows some of the amenities that make our lives comfortable. Electricity and telephone wires often run underground but can be carried on poles and pylons from power stations.

BUILDING FOR STRENGTH

A PLATFORM bridge was one of the earliest human inventions, and was probably first used tens of thousands of years ago. People laid a tree trunk or a single slab of stone across narrow rivers or steep gullies to make travelling across easier. Many modern platform bridges are hollow and made of steel. The model here shows how thin folded sheets make a strong, hollow platform. If you stand on a simple platform bridge, the downward force of your weight makes it sag in the middle. Too much weight can snap a flat wooden plank or crack a stone slab.

Arch bridges, however, as the second project shows, are not flat and they do not sag when loaded. They curve up and over the gap that they span. The Romans were among the first to build arch bridges from many separate stone blocks more than 2,000 years ago. The shape of the bridge holds the stone blocks together. Pushing down on the centre of the bridge creates forces which push outwards so that the load is borne by the supports at either side.

A strong bridge
The Rainhill Bridge spanned the Liverpool and Manchester railway in 1832. It was made by fitting stone blocks around a wooden scaffold. The bridge could support itself when workers hammered the keystone at the very top into place.

MAKE A PLATFORM

You will need: *scissors, stiff card, ruler, pen, 2 boards 20x20cm, modelling clay.*

Your platform is stronger than a platform bridge because it is supported on four sides. Without this support it would sag in the middle.

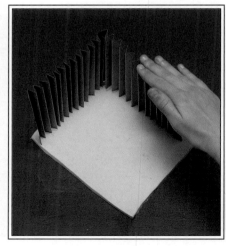

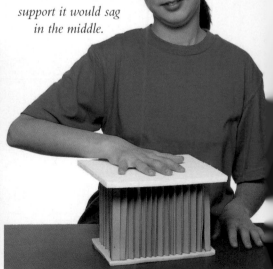

1 Cut out four strips of card 40x10cm. With a ruler and pen, draw lines 1cm apart across each card. Fold each card back and forth across the lines to form zigzag pleats.

2 Lay one board flat on the table. Stand a piece of pleated card upright along the board's edges. Repeat for the other three sides. Use modelling clay to secure each corner.

3 When all sides of the platform are in place, lay the second board on top. Push downwards with your hand. Pleating the card has made the platform very strong.

MAKE AN ARCH

You will need: *2 house-bricks, ruler, sand, 6 wooden toy building blocks, builder's plaster, water, plastic spoon, plastic knife.*

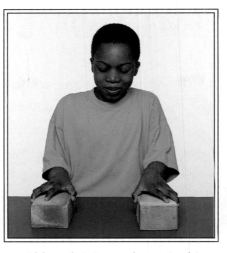

1 Although it is not shown in this picture, it would be a good idea to cover the table with newspaper first of all. Place the two bricks on the table. They should be about 20cm apart.

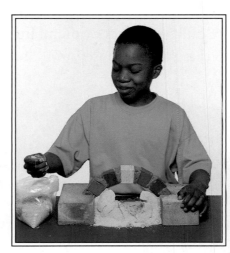

2 Pile up sand between the bricks and smooth it with your hands to make a curved mound. Place the wooden blocks side by side across the sand. The bricks should touch the outer blocks.

3 Notice that the inner blocks touch each other and have V-shaped gaps between them. Mix the plaster with water until it forms a stiff paste. Use the knife to fill the gaps between the blocks with paste.

4 Make sure you have filled each space where the arch meets the bricks. Wait for the plaster to dry. Once dry, remove the sand from underneath the arch.

Like stone blocks in real bridges, the wooden toy blocks make a remarkably strong curve.

5 Push down on the arch and feel how firm it is. The weight that you are putting on the bridge is supported by the two bricks at the side. This bridge is stronger than the platform bridge and does not sag in the middle.

HOME IMPROVEMENTS

Let there be light
This ancient Greek lamp is similar to those people used all over the world for thousands of years to light their homes. Lamps such as this burn olive oil. The flame they give is smoky and not very bright. Candles were also used for lighting in homes as early as 5000BC.

EARLY humans lived in caves or shelters made from stones, wood or earth. They first discovered how to start a fire by rubbing sticks together. Fire provided them with warmth and a way to cook. The earliest houses with permanent walls, roofs and windows were built in villages such as Catal Hüyük in southern Turkey around 8,000 years ago. People there washed with hot water, had fireplaces in the middle of rooms and slept on shelves built against the walls of the houses.

Furniture, such as beds, chairs and tables, was first made by the ancient Egyptians. The ancient Romans built huge public baths and even had central heating 2,000 years ago. The basic design of homes has not changed very much since then. However, houses in Europe did not have chimneys until the 1200s and glass windows were unusual until the 1400s. It was not until the 1800s that many houses were built with indoor plumbing, and electric wiring was not built into the walls of houses until the 1900s.

handle

cistern

water flows down a pipe into the toilet

toilet

Finding the key
Homes need strong locks to keep valuables safe inside. The lock shown in this picture was invented by Joseph Bramah in 1787. It was the safest lock ever invented at the time. He boasted that he would give a reward to anyone who could pick the lock (unlock it without a key). It was 67 years before anyone succeeded.

Flushed with success
The earliest toilets that are known about are more than 4,000 years old. They were found at Harappa and Mohenjo-Daro in Pakistan. Joseph Bramah, who invented the lock, invented the first flush toilet in 1778. This glazed ceramic (pottery) toilet was manufactured in 1850. It used water kept in a cistern (small water tank) above the toilet seat.

1910 vacuum cleaner

1993 vacuum cleaner

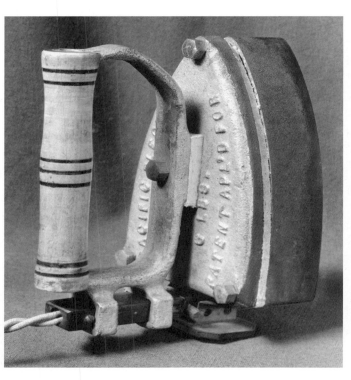

Crisp creases

For over 2,000 years, people have heated flattened pieces of iron to press on to clothes to smooth out wrinkles. In the past, people heated the iron on a fire or on a stove. In the late 1800s, inventors found a way to heat an iron using electricity. This electric iron was first produced in 1903.

Dust buster

Keeping homes clean has always been a concern. Prehistoric people threw their rubbish on to heaps at the edges of villages. In the 1900s, ways of using a vacuum (airless space) to suck in dirt were invented. This early vacuum cleaner, called the Daisy, was first made in 1910. It worked by using a bellows (pump for sucking out air). Modern vacuum cleaners, such as the 1993 Hoover, use power from an electric motor to suck dirt into a bag.

FACT BOX

• People living about 4,500 years ago in the cities of Harappa and Mohenjo-Daro in Pakistan had proper bathrooms in their public buildings. The well-planned cities were built with running water and drains under the streets.

• The oldest known type of lock, called a pin tumbler, is at least 4,000 years old. The oldest example was discovered in Nineveh, Iraq. Locks of this kind were used by the ancient Egyptians and are still used today in some parts of the world.

• Before people in cities had plumbing, they collected waste water in bowls and threw it out of the window into the street. Sometimes the muck fell on other people's heads.

WEAVING

Secret silk
For centuries, weaving silk was a secret known only to the people of China. They learned how to create fine, richly coloured cloth of the kind seen in this banner. It was buried 2,000 years ago.

ALMOST every kind of cloth is made by weaving. Threads made out of plant material such as cotton, or animal fleece such as wool, are woven on a loom. The oldest pieces of cloth known were found in Switzerland and are estimated to be about 7,000 years old. Before people invented ways to make cloth, they wore the skins of the animals they hunted, to keep warm and dry.

The cotton plant grew plentifully in Egypt and India 5,000 years ago. People there invented ways to weave it into clothing. In other parts of the world clothes were made from the wool of sheep or goats. The flax plant was also used to make cloth called linen. In China silk was woven as long as 4,500 years ago. In the 1700s, several inventions made it much easier to spin and weave both cotton and wool thread. These inventions allowed cloth to be made in much larger quantities than ever before. In the 1900s, artificial fibres such as nylon were invented that allowed new kinds of cloth to be made.

Fine thread
Silk is made from the thread that forms the cocoon (covering) spun around themselves by silk moth caterpillars. The cocoons are gathered and washed, and then the thread is unwound. The threads are plaited together to make strong thread for weaving. This Chinese painting from 500 years ago shows women spinning silk thread.

1300s spinning wheel

Spin me a yarn
The plant fibres or animal hair from which most cloth is made have to be spun together to make them strong. This is called yarn. In the 1300s, people in Europe first began to use spinning wheels such as this to spin thread. Experts believe wheels like this were first invented in India about 4,000 years ago.

1769 Arkwright spinning machine

Fast and furious

In the 1700s machines were invented that made it possible to weave cloth far more quickly than before. This meant that thread had to be spun more quickly. In 1769, Richard Arkwright invented a spinning machine that used horse power to turn pulleys and rollers. It spun thread much more quickly than on a spinning wheel.

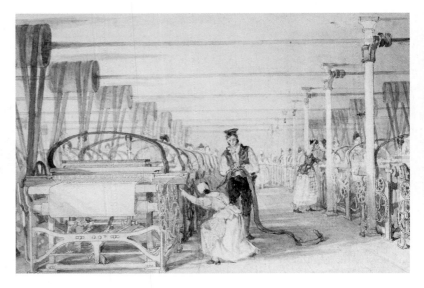

Power weaving

A factory is fitted with some of the first large-scale weaving machines. Large weaving machines powered by steam engines were invented in the 1800s. These machines produced much more cloth than was possible using older ways of weaving. However, the people who looked after the machines in factories like this had to work very long hours in conditions that were often dangerous.

Stretch and bend

Clothes made from wool or plant fibres could be stiff and heavy to wear. Modern clothes made from synthetic fibres are designed to be more comfortable. The clothes this woman is wearing for exercising are made from Lycra, invented in 1953. It is very flexible and ideal to wear when you need to be able to bend.

Lycra

Smooth and shiny

This boy is wearing a raincoat made from polyvinyl chloride (PVC), a kind of plastic invented in 1913. New ways of making material were invented in the 1900s. New kinds of thread called synthetic (artificial) fibre were made from chemicals, not from plants and animal wool. The materials had names such as nylon and polyester.

CLEVER COOKS

People cook food, especially meat, because it kills any germs, which makes it safer to eat. Until about 8,000 years ago the only way to cook meat was by roasting. People pushed a spit (metal rod) through an animal's body and held it over a fire while they turned the meat to cook it all over. The Chinese learned 3,000 years ago how to cook many different kinds of food using the Chinese *wok* (a metal cooking bowl). The ancient Egyptians knew how to bake bread in an oven 5,000 years ago. By the time of the ancient Greeks, people cooked using ovens, saucepans and frying pans. Not surprisingly, the first ever cookery book was written 2,300 years ago by the ancient Greek, Archestratus. Cooking methods changed very little for the next 2,000 years.

Ways of preserving food by freezing were invented in the 1800s and have changed the way people eat. Foods that had only been available in certain seasons could then be eaten all year round. Nowadays people can buy food cooked in advance and heat it up in a few minutes in a microwave oven.

Open-air eating
The Dutch artist Pieter Brueghel the Younger painted village people eating together in the 1500s. The huge cooking pot in the background of the painting was used to cook thick soups or stews over open fires.

Mass catering
In medieval Europe many people lived together in monasteries or castles. Cooking was done in huge kitchens such as this. Large fireplaces made it easier to feed many people quickly. These kitchens continued to be used up until the 1800s, as shown in this drawing of 1816.

Quick cuppa
Tea was first mixed with boiling water as a drink in China 2,000 years ago. It became popular in Europe in the 1600s and is now drunk all over the world. Boiling water in a kettle became much faster in the 1900s when electric kettles like this one were invented.

1921 electric kettle

heat-proof handle

spout

electric element

socket

Long-lasting soup

People have known ways of preserving food (keeping it edible over time) for thousands of years. Meat and fish were salted or dried. Fruit and vegetables were stored in the dark or cooked and then sealed in bottles. In the early 1800s, the Frenchman Nicolas Appert found a new way of keeping food fresh. He sealed it into steel cans, as the men in this factory in the mid-1800s are doing.

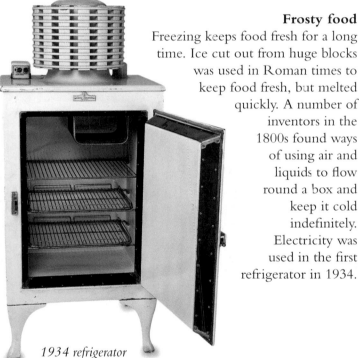

Frosty food

Freezing keeps food fresh for a long time. Ice cut out from huge blocks was used in Roman times to keep food fresh, but melted quickly. A number of inventors in the 1800s found ways of using air and liquids to flow round a box and keep it cold indefinitely. Electricity was used in the first refrigerator in 1934.

1934 refrigerator

Ready in a flash

Microwave ovens cook food faster than any ordinary cooker. Scientists invented this way of using radio waves to heat food in the 1940s. By the 1950s, the first microwave ovens were being sold.

Instant oven

Before the invention of gas cookers, ovens had to be fuelled with wood or coal each morning which meant a lot of hard work. In the 1800s inventors discovered how to make gas from coal and store it safely so that it could be fed through pipes to people's houses. Modern gas cookers like this one are linked up to gas pipes. The owner just turns a valve and gas flows into the cooker where it is lit to provide instant heat for cooking.

YEAST FACTORY

Foaming fermenting whisky!
When yeast is mixed with sugar it creates lots of tiny bubbles. This is called fermentation. When yeast and sugar are mixed together it creates alcohol.

YEAST is a type of fungus that lives on the skins of many fruits. People all over the world have used it for thousands of years for brewing beer and baking bread. Just a spoonful of yeast contains millions of separate single-celled (very simple) organisms. They work like tiny chemical factories, taking in sugar and giving out alcohol and carbon dioxide gas. While they feed, the yeast cells grow larger and then reproduce by splitting in half. Yeast turns grape juice into alcoholic wine and makes beer from mixtures of grain and water. When added to uncooked dough, yeast produces gas bubbles that make the bread light and soft. Brewing and baking are important modern industries that depend on yeast working quickly.

This project consists of four separate experiments. By comparing the results you can discover the best conditions for yeast to grow. Yeast grows best in wet places. Removing the water makes yeast cells dry out and hibernate (sleep). Add water to powdery dried yeast even after many years and it becomes active again.

FINDING THE BEST CONDITIONS

You will need: *measuring jug, water, kettle, sticky coloured labels, 4 small jam jars, teaspoon, dried yeast granules, sugar, scissors, clear film, rubber bands, 2 heatproof bowls, ice cubes.*

1 Half fill a kettle with water. Ask an adult to boil it for you and then put it aside to cool. Boiling the water kills all living organisms that might stop the yeast growing.

2 Label the glass jars one to four. Put a level teaspoonful of dried yeast into each jar as shown here. Then put the same amount of sugar into each jar.

3 Pour 150ml of water into each of the first three jars. Stir the mixture to dissolve the sugar. Do not pour water into the fourth jar. Put this jar away in a warm place.

4 Cut out pieces of clear film about twice a jar's width. Stretch one across the neck of each jar and secure it with a rubber band. Put the first jar in a warm place.

5 Place the second jar in a glass bowl. Put ice cubes and cold water in the bowl. This mixture will keep the jar's temperature close to freezing.

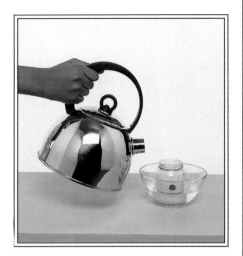

6 Place the third jar in another glass bowl. Pour in hot water that is almost too hot to touch. Take care not to use boiling water or the jar may crack.

7 Regularly check all four jars over the next two hours. As the ice cubes melt, add more to keep the temperature low. Add more hot water to keep the third jar hot.

high temperature   warm temperature   cold temperature   dry jar

8 In the jar that was kept hot, the yeast is a cloudy layer at the bottom, killed by the heat. The yeast in the jar that was kept warm has fed on the water and sugar, and its gas is pushing up the clear film. The jar that was kept cold has only a little froth on the surface because the cold has slowed down the yeast. In the dry jar, there are no signs of activity, although the yeast is mixed with the sugar.

Discoveries in the lab

Alexander Fleming, a Scottish scientist, identified the properties of the Penicillium mould. Chemists working in laboratories try to invent new substances such as plastics, drugs and dyes. They carry out experiments to see what happens when different chemicals and other substances are mixed together. Most of the apparatus (equipment) is made from glass so that the chemists can see what is inside.

STAYING WELL

HUMAN beings have been seeking new ways to cure illness and look after the sick for thousands of years. Today there are many drugs, machines and tools that doctors and nurses can use to fight disease. Yet in some ways little has changed. In ancient Egypt 4,500 years ago, a doctor would use compression (pressure) to stop someone bleeding. A modern doctor would do exactly the same thing. In China 2,000 years ago, doctors knew a great deal about the human body. They also practised a healing technique called acupuncture (inserting needles into parts of the body), which is still used all over the world.

By the 1500s Chinese doctors knew about some of the drugs that we use today. Medicine in the United States and Europe began to develop quickly in the 1800s. Ways were invented to stop germs infecting people and to anaesthetize (make unconscious) patients in surgery. In the 1920s, the British doctor Alexander Fleming discovered, by chance, the first antibiotics (drugs that kill germs). Many more antibiotics have been invented since then which treat different kinds of diseases.

early stethoscopes

Sounds under the skin

The French doctor René Laënnec invented a hollow tube in the early 1800s that allowed him to hear the sounds inside a patient's chest and heart. It was called a stethoscope. Four different kinds can be seen in this photograph. A doctor can find out whether there is illness in a patient's lungs and heart by listening through a stethoscope.

FACT BOX

• The great Indian physician (doctor) Susruta, first discovered that mosquitoes spread malaria and that rats spread plague 1,500 years ago.

• Doctor Willem Kolff invented the first artificial kidney machine in 1943. Like a kidney, the machine removes poisons from a person's bloodstream. People whose kidneys are too damaged to work use this machine.

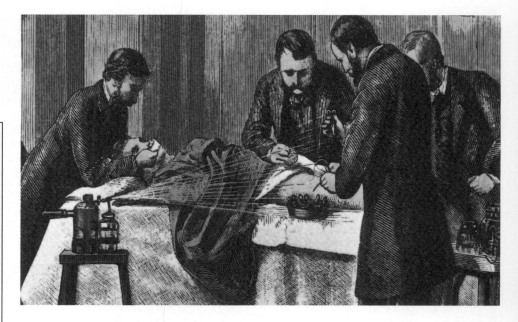

Keeping clean

Surgeons began to use carbolic sprays of the kind shown in this engraving whenever they operated on a patient. Far more people survived surgery because of this. Before the 1800s, many people died after surgery (cutting a body open) because germs infected open wounds. The British surgeon, Joseph Lister, invented a way of preventing this. He washed the wounds in carbolic acid, a chemical that kills germs.

ether inhaler

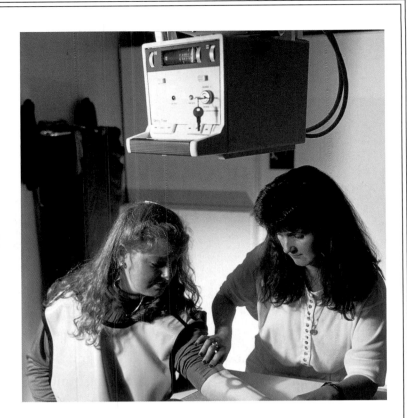

It's a knockout

When surgeons cut people open they are able to give them an anaesthetic (drug that puts people to sleep) to stop them feeling pain. The first modern anaesthetic was discovered in the USA by a dentist, William Morton. In 1846 he used the chemical called ether to stop a patient feeling pain from surgery. Ether inhalers, like the one shown here, were invented to allow patients to breathe in ether before and during an operation.

See-through machine

A radiographer (X-ray specialist) uses an X-ray machine to photograph bones inside a patient's arm. Radiation (radio waves that pass through the air) from the machine passes through the patient and strikes a piece of film leaving a picture of her bones. The German scientist Wilhelm Konrad von Röntgen discovered this special radiation by accident in 1895.

Just a pinprick

Many drugs are given by injecting them into a person's vein or muscle using a hypodermic syringe. Usable syringes were invented in the 1600s but they carried germs. In 1869 the French scientist Luer invented the first all-glass syringe. This was easier to keep germ-free. Disposable syringes became available in the 1970s.

Beating heart

Modern electrocardiographs (ECGs) such as this one can be used in hospitals everywhere to check patients' heartbeats and warn of heart disease. The Dutch scientist Willem Einthoven invented a way of recording the beating of people's hearts as a line on a piece of paper in 1901. However, his machine was very large and heavy. He was awarded the Nobel Prize for his achievement in 1924.

reel spin freely.

PROJECT

ON THE WIRE

NTIL about 200 years ago, the best way to send a message was to write a letter and give it to a rider on a fast horse. In 1838 the American, Samuel Morse, invented an electric telegraph that could send messages over a wire. Morse installed the first telegraph line between Washington and Baltimore in 1844. The first telegraph cable to span the Atlantic Ocean was laid in 1866. Some people have called the telegraph the Victorian Internet. Morse also invented a special code to use with his telegraph. The code is just like an alphabet, but instead of symbols there are long and short bursts of electricity that make blips of sound.

You can make your own telegraph and use it to communicate with a friend. There are two symbols used in telegraph communication, a dot (.) and a dash (–). Each letter of the alphabet is represented by a different group of dots and dashes.

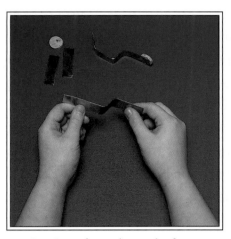

1 Cut 2cm from the end of each copper strip. Bend the longer strips to the shape shown here. Glue a circle of cork to one end.

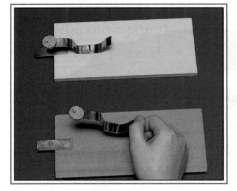

2 Use a drawing pin to fix 2cm copper strip to each baseboard. Fix one copper strip with the cork to each of the baseboards. Position the cork just over the edge of the board.

MAKE A TELEGRAPH

You will need: *scissors, 2 flexible copper strips 10x10cm, strong glue, 2 cork circles, 4 drawing pins, 2 pieces of fibreboard 16x8cm, screwdriver, 2 bulb holders with screws to fix, 2 bulbs, 2 batteries with holders, 2 paper clips, plastic-covered wire.*

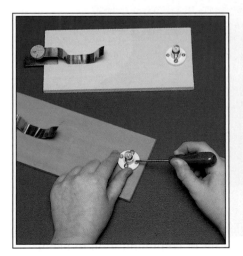

3 Fix each bulb holder to the opposite end of the baseboard. Using a screwdriver, turn the screws clockwise to make them bite into the baseboard.

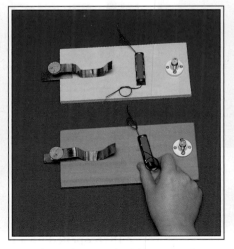

4 Glue a battery holder to each baseboard. Position it midway between the rear of the copper strip and the bulb holder. Remove 1cm of insulation from each of the wires.

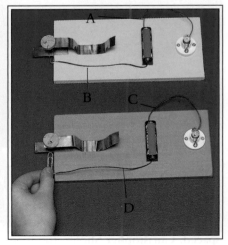

5 Attach the red wires (A and C) to the bulb screws as shown here. Attach the black wires (B and D) to the 2cm copper strip with a paper clip.

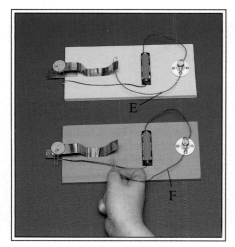

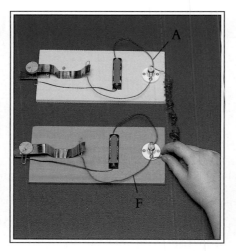

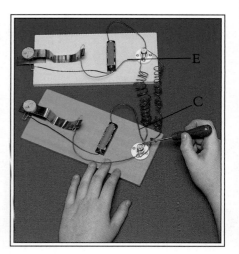

6 Use more wire to connect the rear end of each copper strip to one side of each bulb holder (wires E and F). Tighten the terminals on the holders to make a good connection.

7 Using a length of wire at least a metre long connect wire A to wire F. Make sure the wires are tightly connected.

8 With an equal length of wire connect wire C to wire E as shown here. Again, make sure the wires are tightly conected.

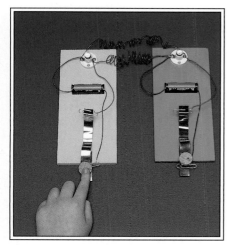

9 The telegraphs are now connected. Press one of the corks down to test whether your telegraph works. Both lights should light up.

10 To make a dash with your telegraph hold down the cork for half a second and to make a dot hold the cork down for a quarter of a second. Now you can try sending messages to a friend. Remember that your partner will have to look up each letter, so leave gaps when sending letters.

Slow talking
A telegraphist of the 1880s could send and receive about 80 letters of the alphabet each minute, which would be about 12 to 15 words a minute. You speak at the rate of about 200 to 300 words a minute.

WARNING!
Please take care when using electrical equipment. Always have an adult present.

WORLD OF SOUND

P EOPLE communicate by sound when they talk to one another, but if they are too far apart, they cannot hear each other. The discovery in the 1800s that it is possible to send sounds over long distances changed people's lives. It allowed them to speak to one another even though they were hundreds of miles apart. Sound can be carried long distances in two ways, along wires or through the air. When Alexander Graham Bell invented the first telephone in 1876, he used wires to send sound. Telephones continued to use wires for many years. In the late 1800s, the Italian Guglielmo Marconi invented a device that sent sounds through the air. It was called radio. Today people all over the world communicate by radio. In the 1800s, machines were also invented that allowed people to store sound so that it could be played back after it had been recorded. The first sound recorder, invented by Thomas Edison in 1877, was called a phonograph. In the mid–1900s, ways were invented to record sound on to tape and plastic compact discs (CDs).

Radio genius

Guglielmo Marconi uses the radio equipment he invented. In 1901 he travelled to Newfoundland in Canada and there received the first transatlantic radio message. This proved that messages could be sent by radio over distances as great as the 4,800km between Europe and America.

Sound bites

On early phonographs such as this 1903 machine the sound was recorded on to a wax-coated cylinder. Each cylinder could only play for three to four minutes. In spite of this, phonographs became very popular.

radio waves

aerial

aerial

radio station

radio

Carried on the air

Sounds such as the human voice are turned into electricity inside a microphone. The electric signal is then transmitted by an aerial as radio waves through the air. These waves travel to an aerial that passes the signal to a radio. The radio can be tuned to turn the signal back into sounds that people can hear.

Sound decorating

By the 1920s radios and speakers such as this were being made for use in the home. The radio, which was finished in a black textured metal case, was orginally designed for use on polar expeditions. The speaker however, was designed to be as beautiful as a piece of furniture.

The Golden Age

By the 1930s, radio had become an entertainment medium (a way of communicating) that broadcast news and music all over the world. People often called the radio the "wireless" because it was not joined to the transmitting station by wires. Millions listened in on radio sets, like the one shown here, to national radio networks such as the BBC in the UK and NBC in the USA.

Cool sounds

This type of radio became very popular in the 1950s. It used transistors, which are tiny electronic components that amplify (strengthen) weak radio signals. Transistor radios were also quite small and therefore portable. The transistor was invented in 1948 and is now used in many electronic devices.

Dramatically vivid discs

This DVD (Digital Video Disc) player offers a richness of sound and clarity of picture not previously available in other machines. Like a CD (compact disc) player, it uses a laser to scan across the surface of a plastic disc. The digitally recorded sounds on the disc are then fed into earphones through which the user listens.

LISTEN TO THIS

SOUND is energy that moves back and forth through the air as vibrations. These vibrations spread outwards as waves, like the ripples caused by a stone dropped into a still lake. Inventors have created ways to communicate by chanelling these sounds.

In the first part of this project, you can see how sound waves can be made to travel in a particular direction. Channelling the sound inside a tube concentrates the waves in the direction of the tube. By channelling sound towards a candle, you can use the energy to blow out the flame. The second part of this project shows how sound is a form of energy. Loud sounds carry large amounts of energy. Scientists say that loud sounds have large amplitudes (strengths). The last part investigates pitch (frequency of vibration). Low sounds consist of a small number of vibrations every second. Musicians say low sounds have low pitch but scientists say they have low frequency. You can make a set of panpipes and see how pitch depends on the length of each pipe.

Play it again, Sam!
You can play deep notes or low notes on a guitar. The sound waves vibrate slowly with a frequency as low as 50 times each second, high notes vibrate much more rapidly.

HOW SOUND TRAVELS

You will need: *clear film, tube of card, elastic band, candle, matches.*

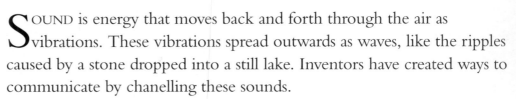

1 Stretch the clear film tightly over the end of the tube. Use the elastic band to fasten it in place. You could also use a flat piece of rubber cut from a balloon.

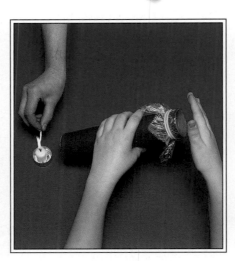

2 Ask an adult to light the candle. Point the tube at the candle, with the open end 10cm from the flame. Give the clear film a sharp tap with the flat of your hand.

3 You hear the sound coming out of the tube. It consists of pressure waves in the air. The tube concentrates the sound waves towards the candle flame and puts it out.

SOUND WAVES

You will need: *clockwork watch, tube 5cm x 1m long.*

1 Place the watch close to your ear. You can hear a ticking sound coming from it. The sound becomes fainter when you move the watch away from your ear.

2 Place one end of the tube to a friend's ear and hold the watch at the other. The tube concentrates the sound and does not let it spread out. She can hear the watch clearly.

HOW TO MAKE PANPIPES

You will need: *scissors, wide drinks straws, modelling clay, card, sticky tape.*

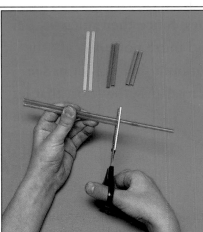

1 Cut the straws so that you have pairs that are 9cm, 8cm, 7cm, and 6cm long. Block one end of each straw with a small piece of modelling clay.

2 Carefully cut out the card to the same shape as the blue piece shown above. Tape the straws into place with the modelling clay along the most slanted edge.

3 Gently blow across the tops of the straws. You will find that the longer pipes produce lower notes than the shorter pipes. The longer pipes have a lower pitch and the shorter pipes have a higher pitch.

BLOW UP

lens

screw

Inner world
Van Leeuwenhoek's microscope had a spike and a glass lens on a flat sheet. He stuck the object he wanted to view on the spike and turned the screw to bring the object opposite the lens. Then he turned the microscope over and looked through the lens.

THE earliest microscope was invented by the Dutch scientist Antoni van Leeuwenhoek around 1660. It contained a single round glass lens about the size of a raindrop.

If you look at an ordinary magnifying glass you will see that the two surfaces curve slightly. The curved surfaces bend light as it travels from the object to your eye. A window pane has two flat surfaces and so does not act as a magnifying glass. Powerful magnifying glasses have highly curved surfaces. Van Leeuwenhoek realized that a glass sphere has the maximum possible curvature. As a result, a spherical lens has the maximum possible magnification of about 300 times. The invention of this microscope opened up a whole new world. For the first time, people could see pollen grains from flowers, bacteria and the sperm from male animals. In this project you can make a copy of van Leeuwenhoek's microscope by using a tiny droplet of water instead of a glass sphere.

JAM JAR MICROSCOPE

You will need: *two large jam jars, water, a pencil.*

2 Find the position that gives the clearest image with the greatest magnification.

1 Fill a jam jar with water and place it at the edge of a table. Look through the jar with one eye and move the pencil back and forth behind the jam jar.

3 Place a second water-filled jam jar close behind the first one. Hold the pencil in the water in the second jar. Move the pencil back and forth.

4 You will find that the image is about four or five times larger than before.

WATER DROP MAGNIFIER

You will need: *aluminium milk bottle cap, metal spoon, candle, small nail, water, flower.*

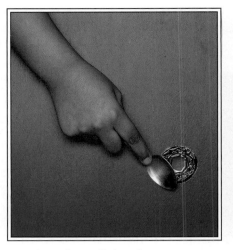

1 Place the milk bottle cap on a hard surface. Use the outer bowl of a spoon to flatten the cap. Stroke the spoon from side to side until the centre of the cap is flat and smooth.

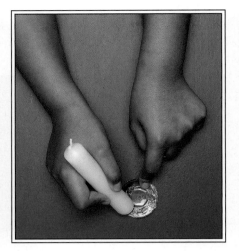

2 Rub the milk bottle cap on both sides with the end of a candle. Make certain that both sides of the smooth centre part are coated with a thin layer of wax.

3 Push the nail through the centre of the milk bottle cap to make a small hole in it. The hole should be perfectly round and measure about 2mm across.

4 Collect water on a fingertip so that a droplet hangs down. Hold the cap flat and lower the drop on to the hole. The wax holds the water in a round lens shape.

5 To use your magnifier, hold it about 1 to 2cm from the object. Now bring your eye as close to the water droplet as possible. Look at how the flower is magnified.

The world in a grain of sand

This woman is using van Leeuwenhoek's simple microscope by pressing it against her eye. Unlike most later microscopes, this was not a heavy instrument which could not be moved easily but a light, portable object. By using this microscope scientists were able to discover much more about the world around us, including the insides of our own bodies.

PICTURE SHOWS

A SIMPLE form of photography began almost 2,000 years ago. The ancient Greeks discovered that light passing through a small hole in the wall of a dark room would make an image in the room of what was outside. In the 1500s, scientists discovered the same happened if a tiny hole was made in a completely dark room. They called the room a *camera obscura*. In the early 1800s scientists tried to find a way to permanently record the image this box made. If they were successful, it would mean that they could make pictures of the world without drawing or painting. The scientists put lenses into their cameras to sharpen the image. In 1840 William Fox Talbot invented a way of coating paper with light-sensitive chemicals that recorded the camera's image permanently.

By the late 1800s Thomas Edison had invented a camera that could record motion, and a kinetoscope, a machine that could project moving pictures. By the beginning of the 1900s, motion pictures were being made and shown commercially. Now cinema is one of the biggest forms of entertainment in the world.

Box of tricks
This early camera was so large and cumbersome that the user needed a handcart to carry it in. The extra equipment is for developing the photographs. This camera dates from the 1850s.

Silver light
Photographs like this portrait of the English inventor Michael Faraday with his wife were made in the mid-1800s. They are known as daguerrotypes after their inventor, Louis Daguerre. They were made on small sheets of copper coated with a light-sensitive layer of silver.

Positive outlook
The images in most cameras are made on to negatives. From these, the positives (the prints) are made. Using negatives means many prints can be made from one negative. The Polaroid camera shown here was invented in the 1940s. It was called an instant camera because it produced a positive image immediately.

Polaroid camera

Freeze-frame gallops

The first accurate photographs of an animal in motion were taken by the English photographer Eadweard Muybridge. While in California in 1877, Muybridge was asked by a horse trainer to take pictures of a racehorse. The trainer wanted to prove for a bet that all four of a galloping horse's legs came off the ground at the same time for a split second during the gallop. As these photographs show, the trainer was correct.

The full works

Two French brothers, August and Louis Lumière, invented this camera for moving pictures in 1895. It was both a camera and a projector and so was much better than Edison's early kinetoscope. The brothers called their invention a *cinématographe*, which has given us the modern word cinema.

cinématographe

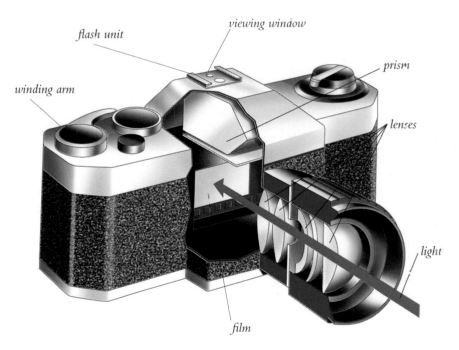

flash unit

viewing window

prism

winding arm

lenses

light

film

Reflex action

Single lens reflex (SLR) cameras became very popular after they were first developed in the 1930s. Light enters the camera through the lenses at the front and strikes the negative at the back. Users can see clearly what they are photographing by means of a prism mounted in the camera.

Picture by numbers

Digital cameras receive light through a lens in the same way as ordinary cameras. The difference in a digital camera is that the light, instead of striking a piece of plastic film, is digitally recorded by light sensors. The digital information is then stored inside the camera and can be played back on a computer screen.

WINDOW ON THE WORLD

Once Guglielmo Marconi had invented a way to broadcast sound and people became interested in radio, inventors soon tried to find a way to broadcast pictures. John Logie Baird, a Scottish inventor, set himself the task of achieving this. Unfortunately no one else believed it was possible to broadcast pictures and he was forced to work alone and in great poverty.

In 1926, Baird finally succeeded in sending a picture a few metres, but his way of sending pictures was not perfect. In the 1930s Vladimir Zworykin, a Russian electrical engineer, invented a better way to send pictures by using electricity to run through a cathode ray tube. Zworykin's invention was essential for modern television. The first public television programmes were broadcast by the BBC in Britain in 1936, and by the 1950s, televisions were beginning to appear in every home in the United States and Europe.

dummy *disc* *electric motor*

Spinning circle
The first picture to be captured as electrical impulses was a dummy's head. Baird placed three discs with holes in them in front of the dummy. These created flashing patterns of light that were turned into electrical impulses by a photoelectric cell (device for turning light into electricity).

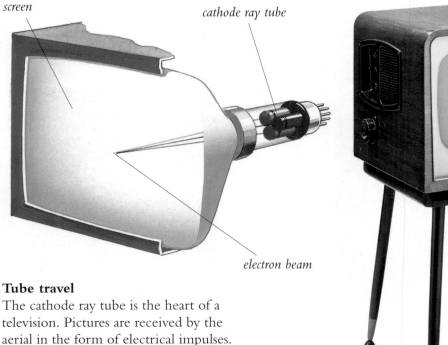

screen *cathode ray tube*

electron beam

1950s television

Tube travel
The cathode ray tube is the heart of a television. Pictures are received by the aerial in the form of electrical impulses. These impulses control a stream of electrons inside the cathode ray tube. The electron beam scans across the screen and creates the picture as points of coloured light. This is the picture that the viewer sees.

Box in the corner
The televisions that large numbers of people first began to buy in the 1950s looked very much like this one. The screens were small and the pictures could only be seen as black-and-white images. Reception was also difficult because there were very few transmitters.

Light in the gloom

When television was first widely broadcast, people saw it as something very new. Most programmes were broadcast only in the evenings and families gathered together to enjoy this new form of entertainment. Gradually more and more people bought televisions.

Moving eye

The cameras used in modern television studios are much more complicated devices than John Logie Baird's invention. This camera is on wheels and can move around the people or objects being filmed. It can move in closer and tilt up or down. Inside the camera, the image is changed into electrical impulses.

Super cool

Modern television screens are much bigger than those available in the 1950s and most are in colour. Flat-screen televisions, such as this one, first became available in the early 1990s. These televisions do not have cathode-ray tubes. Liquid crystals display the picture on the screen.

SCREEN SCENES

THE picture on a television screen is made up from thin lines of light. Follow the instructions in this project and you will also see that the picture consists of just three colours – red, green and blue. Viewed from a distance, these colours mix to produce the full range of colours that we see naturally around us. A TV picture is just rows of glowing dots of coloured light. Fax machines work in a similar way to TV, only more slowly. Feed a sheet of paper into a fax machine and a beam of light moves back and forth across it. Dark places absorb the light and pale places reflect it. The reflected light enters a detector that produces an electric current. The strength of the current depends on the intensity of the reflected light. The electric current is changed into a code made up from chirping sounds that travel down the line to the receiving fax machine. The code controls a scanner that moves across heat-sensitive paper and produces a *facsimile* (copy) of the original. The last part of this project shows how a fax machine breaks an image into tiny areas that are either black or white.

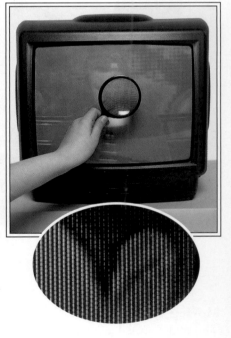

Fast messages
A fax machine sends pictures or writing down the phone line to another fax machine in seconds. The first fax machine was invented in 1904 by the German physicist Arthur Korn. They became common in the 1980s but they are slowly being replaced by electronic e-mail.

LOOKING AT A TV PICTURE

You will need: TV set, torch, powerful magnifying glass.

1 Turn off the TV. Shine the torch close to the screen and look through the magnifying glass. You will see that the screen is covered in very fine lines.

2 Turn on the TV and view the screen through the lens. The picture is made up of minute rectangles of light coloured red, green or blue.

SECONDARY COLOURS

You will need: *red, green, and blue transparent plastic film, 3 powerful torches, 3 rubber bands, white card.*

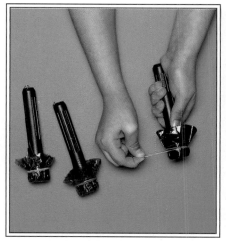

1 Attach a piece of coloured film over the end each torch. Stretch the film tightly and use a rubber band to hold it firmly in place.

2 Shine the torches on to the white card. You can see the three different primary colours of – red, green and blue.

3 Position the torches so that the three circles of coloured light overlap in a cloverleaf pattern. Overlapping colours mix to give new colours.

DIGITAL IMAGES

You will need: *ruler, tracing paper, photograph, black felt pen.*

2 The digitized image contains less detail than the original photo. You could increase the detail by using a greater number of smaller squares.

1 Rule lines 5mm apart to cover the tracing paper in squares. Put the paper over the photograph. Use the pen to fill each dark square. Leave each light square.

The picture is made from squares that are either black or white.

RAW MATERIALS

Human beings have learned over thousands of years that it is possible to change raw materials so that they can be used. Between 6,000 and 3,500 years ago people discovered that they could obtain metals such as copper and iron by heating ore (rock that contains metals). The metals were then heated and shaped to make tools, weapons and ornaments. Metals are still used all over the world to make millions of useful objects.

Another breakthrough in the use of natural resources was grinding flour to bake in an oven to make bread. The Chinese discovered 2,000 years ago that tree bark, old rags and rope could be made into a pulp and then dried to make paper. In the 1800s, from rocks deep in the earth, oil was discovered as a new source of energy. Later, people learned how to use oil to make plastics and other synthetics. Today oil is the greatest single raw material used throughout the world.

The age of bronze
About 6,000 years ago, in what is now the Middle East, people first learned how to mix metals to make an alloy. They dug up ores that contained copper and tin, and smelted them together. From this new metal they created tools and weapons such as this sword. Bronze was much more useful than pure copper because it lasted longer and could be sharpened repeatedly. Gradually, other people in Europe and the Mediterranean world learned how to make bronze.

Mysterious knowledge
Lead cannot be turned into gold, but during medieval times many people such as this alchemist believed that it was possible. An alchemist drew on his knowledge of chemistry and magic to try turning lead into gold. People feared the alchemists were magicians. Although the alchemists never made gold from lead, they did pave the way for modern chemistry.

A taste of steel
The Bessemer converter marked a new way of making steel in the mid-1800s. The British inventor Sir Henry Bessemer had been making cannon out of iron for use in the Crimean War when he had the idea for the converter. Air is blown into molten iron inside the converter taking away any impurities and creating strong steel for use in many different industries.

Brand-new material

In the early 1900s, the chemist Leo Baekeland invented a way of creating a thick liquid from chemicals which, when it hardened, became a new material that no one had ever seen before. He called this material Bakelite. It was long lasting and could be shaped to make many different kinds of objects such as this radio case.

Strong and light

In the late 1800s, the electrolytic cell was invented as a way of using electricity to extract the light, strong metal called aluminium from bauxite ore. Aluminium is used when strong, light metal is needed, for example in building aircraft.

Riding on air

When motor cars were invented in the late 1800s their wheels were hard, like cartwheels. Charles Goodyear invented a process that made rubber hard and allowed people to make car tyres from it. Inside the tyres were inner tubes filled with air, which were first invented in 1845 by Robert Thomson.

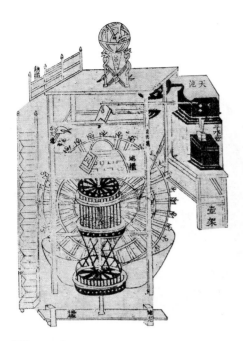

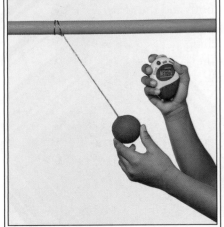

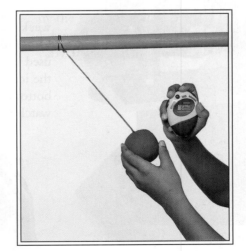

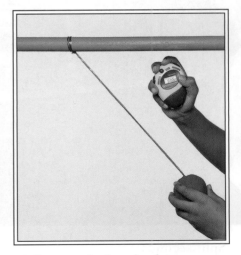

RIVER OF TIME

THE Ancient Egytians invented water clocks in about 3000BC because the sundials they used could not tell the time at night. Water clocks use water that slowly drips from a bowl and the level of the surface of the remaining water indicates the time. However, a water clock cannot tell the time until you have compared it with another clock. You can make a water clock in the second part of this project.

In 1581, the Italian Galileo Galilei studied how different pendulums swinging back and forth could indicate time. He discovered that the time depends only on the length of the pendulum. It is not affected by the mass of the pendulum, or how far it swings from side to side. You can repeat Galileo's important experiment in the first part of this project. In 1641, Galileo's son Vincenzio Galilei constructed a mechanical clock that used a weighted pendulum to control the speed of hands across a clockface. All grandfather and grandmother clocks work like this. However, pendulums are not always accurate because their speed can vary depending on changes such as heat.

Water timer

This Chinese water clock was built in 1088. Water trickles into tiny buckets fixed to the outside of a large wheel. As each bucket fills up, the wheel clicks round to the next empty bucket. Each bucket empties as it reaches the lowest position. The position of the wheel indicates the time.

MAKE A PENDULUM

You will need: *modelling clay, string, stopwatch.*

1 Roll some clay to make a ball 4cm across. Use string to hang it 30cm below a support. Pull the ball out to the position shown. Let go and time 10 complete swings.

2 Repeat the experiment. This time, use a larger heavier ball with the same bit of string. You will find that the time for ten swings is the same despite the heavier ball.

3 Increase the length of your pendulum by hanging the ball from a longer piece of string. You will find that the pendulum swings more slowly than before.

MAKE A WATER CLOCK

You will need: *bradawl, aluminium pie dish, drinking straw, large plastic tumbler, scissors, water jug, marker.*

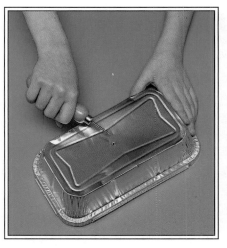

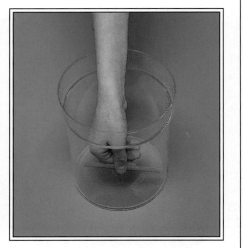

1 Use the bradawl to make a small hole in the bottom of the pie dish. The smaller the hole, the longer your water clock will run.

2 Place the drinking straw in the bottom of the plastic tumbler. It will act as a pointer as the water level rises. Cut the straw with a pair of scissors if it is too long.

3 Place the pie dish on top of the plastic tumbler. Make sure the hole in the pie dish is over the centre of the tumbler.

4 Pour water from a jug into the pie dish. Keep adding water until the dish is full. As soon as water starts to fall into the tumbler, note the time on your watch.

5 After 10 minutes, use the marker to mark the water level on the side of the tumbler. As the water drips into the tumbler, mark the level at 10-minute intervals.

You can use your pie-dish water clock to time your eggs for breakfast.

6 After half an hour you have three marks up the side of the tumbler. Empty out the water, refill the pie dish and you can use your water clock to measure time passing.

CROSSING THE OCEANS

Over the centuries, people have developed ways of crossing the vast seas and oceans of the world. On board ships were pilots, navigators and captains whose job it was to navigate (find directions) across the water and arrive in one particular place. Even from the time of the earliest ship we know of, built for an Egyptian prince's funeral 6,000 years ago, seamen tried to find their way by looking at the position of the stars in the night sky and the sun during the day.

However, it is difficult to calculate exactly where you are from looking at the stars without working out complicated sums using angles and numbers. Over the years a number of instruments such as compasses and octants were invented to help seamen navigate. Maps also helped people to find their way at sea. Early maps did not have very much information. As ever more people travelled to distant places, more detailed maps were drawn of different regions and seas.

Star wheels
The astrolabe, invented by the ancient Greeks, was used for centuries to find directions at sea. The lower disc has a map of the stars and the upper disc has lines showing the heights of stars. This astrolabe dates from the AD1000s.

Looking north
The compass is still one of the most widely used, simple instruments that help people find directions. Chinese and European seamen discovered 700 years ago that a tiny piece of magnetic stone floated on water will always turn towards the Pole Star in the north. Sailors began taking instruments containing pieces of magnetic stone or metal to sea with them. This one dates from the 1300s and the decoration on the top of the compass face shows the direction north.

Charting the seas
Without knowing distances accurately it is very difficult to plan a journey. Making maps of large distances is difficult because the earth is round and maps are flat. It was not until the 1500s that Gerardus Mercator found a way to draw maps like this one of Iceland. It represented the distances on the surface of the earth. Using maps of this kind, travellers could find their way more easily than before.

1761 octant

adjustable screw

Degree course
Sea captains in the 1600s and 1700s used instruments such as this octant to observe stars. By holding the octant upright and looking through it at a star, the captain could move the vertical bar along the curved bar at the bottom. The distance moved along the curved bar told the captain how high the star was from the horizon.

curved base bar

graduated eighths of a circle

Rush for a cuppa
By the 1800s, sea navigation was so highly developed that it was possible to predict how long a ship's journey would take. Very fast ships such as this tea clipper, which carried valuable tea from India, raced one another in the 1860s to see who could make the round trip from India to Britain in the shortest time.

Deep sea hunter
Modern submarines can remain submerged under water for months. Finding directions underwater is even more difficult than on the surface so submarines use a number of ways to navigate. As well as using compasses and maps, they communicate with global positioning satellites (GPS) by radio. The satellites in space send back messages to tell the submarines where they are.

Spectacular sport
Sailing is now a very popular sport and many people all over the world sail boats such as this trimaran for pleasure and in races. Every boat must carry charts, a modern compass and a direction-finding radio before it is considered safe to sail in.

DRIVING AHEAD

THE invention of the wheel was one of the most important technological advances that human beings ever made. It allowed them to travel and transport heavy weights on vehicles pulled by animals such as oxen and horses. Experts believe that knowledge of how to make wheels first developed almost 6,000 years ago in what is now the Middle East. It then spread gradually to people in neighbouring regions. In China, wheels were first made about 3,000 years ago. Some civilizations such as the Aztec and Mayan cultures in America never discovered how to make wheels. Until the invention of the steam engine in the 1800s, wheeled transport could not travel any faster than a horse could gallop. Once steam trains had been invented in the early 1800s, people began to travel faster and faster on land. Early motor cars were very slow because their engines were small and inefficient. However, as engines became bigger, cars travelled faster and faster too.

Flying squad
One immediate effect of discovering the wheel was a revolution in warfare. Racing down on their enemies in a horse-drawn chariot like this one gave the Egyptians a great advantage. War chariots were very light and fast.

FACT BOX

• The world's fastest train is the French *Train à Grande Vitesse*. It travels at speeds up 300kph during normal journeys, but it is capable of reaching 500kph.

• The diesel engine is named after Rudolf Diesel, who invented it in 1892. Modern diesel engines power cars, trucks and trains.

Pull and push
The first wheels were solid and made out of pieces of wood cut and joined together. Gradually wheels were made lighter and stronger. The spoked wheel on this medieval wagon was the strongest kind of wheel. The spokes absorbed shocks from the wheel as it turned.

Stage by stage
In the 1800s huge numbers of people travelled to the American West when it opened up for settlement. The country was very wild and, until the railroads were built in the 1870s, stagecoaches like this were the only form of public transport. They were very uncomfortable to travel in because they pitched and swayed over rocks and holes in the badly made roads.

First of many

The invention of the steam engine changed the face of transport forever. George Stephenson's *Rocket*, shown here, was built in 1829 and was one of the first steam locomotives. He built it with his son for the Manchester–Liverpool Railway. By the late 1800s, railways stretched all over Europe, North America and much of Asia.

On the cheap

Henry Ford's Model T was the first motor car designed to be built in huge numbers very cheaply. Earlier cars had been hand-made and so were expensive, but Ford designed a system that made it possible to build cheaper cars on an assembly line in a factory. By the time the last Model T came out of the factory in 1927, 15 million had been built since 1908.

Electric engine

Steam railway engines using coal were built in their thousands throughout the 1800s. The first electric locomotives, like this one in Britain, were built in the early 1900s. They were quieter and cleaner than steam engines so they slowly replaced them.

Flash motor

Some of the earliest cars were built by Karl Benz in the late 1800s. He founded a factory that expanded to become the company that built this modern car. This Mercedes–Benz S430L can travel at a top speed of 240 kph. It is equipped with modern safety features such as airbags and uses tiny computers that control the car's stability and braking.

FLYING HIGH

Birds and insects fly by using their wings to lift off the ground and support their weight on currents of air. Although humans have never had wings, they have always wanted to fly like birds. Scientists and inventors looked for ways to make artificial wings for hundreds of years.

Kites were invented in China 2,000 years ago and may have been used for military purposes. In the 1780s, the Montgolfier brothers flew in balloons over France. Balloons, however, proved too difficult to steer to be practical. Powered flight has only been possible in the past hundred years. The Wright brothers flew their first aeroplane in 1903, in the USA, and showed that it is possible to control the movement of an aircraft. Like the invention of the wheel, the discovery of flight changed warfare. Air power was used in war only 11 years after the Wright brothers' first flight. Commercial air travel became more and more popular from the 1960s onward.

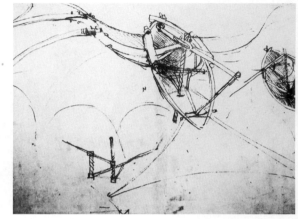

Bird man
The Italian artist and inventor Leonardo da Vinci drew designs for flying machines in the early 1500s. This drawing shows wings that could be strapped to the arms to allow the wearer to fly. However, they were never built.

Keep going
This is one of the Wright brothers' first aircraft, the first successful flying machine. One engine attached to the frame turned propellers and created enough power to keep the aircraft moving forward. This provided the essential lift from air rushing past under and over the wings to keep it airborne.

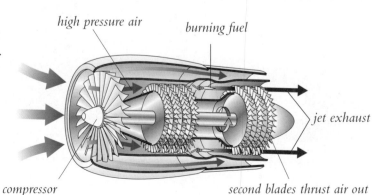

Blades of power
A jet turbine takes in air through the front blades. As the blades turn faster they compress the air which is ignited. The second blades are moved by the burning air which then turns the compressor. This drives the aircraft on.

high pressure air

burning fuel

jet exhaust

compressor

second blades thrust air out

Whirly bird
The man sitting at the controls of this early helicopter is the Russian-born Igor Sikorsky. After 1917, he went to live in the USA and worked as an aeroplane engineer. By 1940, he had developed the first successful vertical take-off helicopter and flew several of the early machines he built.

Flying boat
The largest commercial aircraft built between World War I and World War II were flying boats of the kind shown here. Because there were few long runways built on land, large planes often took off from, and landed on, water. This six-engined plane flew on routes between Italy and South America.

Two in one
The Harrier jump-jet is a unique type of aircraft. It can land and take off vertically like a helicopter, but it flies like a jet. The aircraft has movable jet thrusters that are vertical when landing and taking off but horizontal when in flight. This type of aircraft is mainly used for military purposes.

Wide blue yonder
The Space Shuttle is the ultimate aircraft. It takes off vertically attached to rocket boosters, to reach orbit around the Earth. When it returns from orbit, the Shuttle glides through the atmosphere and lands just like any jet plane.

Jetsetter
The de Havilland *Comet* shown here was the first jet aircraft to go into regular passenger service. It began flying in 1952 and halved the time for long journeys such as that between London and South Africa. By 1958, regular jet flights between Britain and the USA meant transatlantic jet travel had come to stay.

NUMBER CRUNCHERS

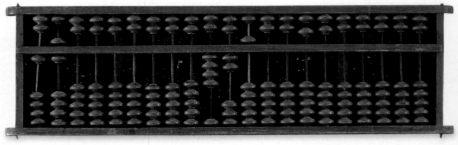

It is not certain exactly when people first invented numbers. We do know, however, that numbers were in use by the time the first civilizations grew up, 6,000 years ago. In these early societies, numbers allowed people to count possessions when trading and to note the days of the week and months of the year. The Greek inventor Hero of Alexandria designed a counting machine 2,000 years ago and, in the early 1500s, Leonardo da Vinci also designed one. In 1835 Charles Babbage invented a mechanical calculator called the difference engine. A mechanical calculator was later used to break codes (secret communications) during World War II. These machines were the first computers. Afterwards, ever larger electronic computers were built, and in the 1980s small personal computers (PCs) appeared in offices and at home.

Counter culture
People have been using this kind of counting device for thousands of years. It is known in China as a *suan pan* and as an abacus in English. Beads are arranged on vertical, parallel strings. Each string represents different kinds of number. For example, on the extreme left are 1s, next left 10s. By sliding the beads up and down, a person can quickly perform complicated arithmetic.

Brass and steel
The difference engine is a complicated arrangement of metal cogs and ratchets designed to count numbers mechanically. It was invented by Charles Babbage in 1835 but he never succeeded in finishing it. Building such a machine out of solid metal parts without any electrical circuits is extremely difficult.

Code breaker
Colossus was the name given to this computer built at Bletchley in Britain during World War II. It was used to break codes used by German commanders who sent orders by radio. The orders were sent as constantly changing groups of letters that only made sense to those who knew the key. *Colossus* performed the millions of calculations necessary to read the code even though the British did not have the key.

Micro-maze

Silicon chips allow modern computers to perform millions of calculations in a second. Before chips were invented, enormous boxes were needed to hold all the wires required to calculate electronically. Then miniaturization was invented. This made it possible to put many tiny circuits on to one piece of silicon.

Carry on computing

A small computer can be carried and used anywhere. Batteries inside supply power for the hardware. Portable computers are often called laptops because they are small and light enough to place on a sitting person's lap.

A boring box

This very uninteresting looking box is in fact one of the world's fastest computers. There is little to look at on the outside because everything interesting is inside, where thousands of chips can calculate trillions of numbers every second.

Out into space

To operate in space without human help, spacecraft such as the *Voyager* probe are equipped with computers that control them. Without small computers, spacecraft would never be able to leave earth. They would need to carry machines to control them so large that the spacecraft would weigh far too much to leave the earth's surface.

THROUGH THE LOGIC GATE

INFORMATION flowing inside a computer is called data. It is in the form of electrical pulses. Data changes as it passes through part of the computer called the central processing unit (CPU). The CPU has thousands of separate high-speed switches called logic gates. These logic gates are microscopic transistors cut into a silicon chip. They can flick on and off up to 300 million times a second. Data flows into the input side of each gate. It only flows out again if the gate is switched on. The computer program sets up how the gates switch on and off and so controls the data flow through the computer.

There are three main types of gates, called AND, NOT, and OR gates. Working together, they act as counters or memory circuits to store data. Logic gates are also used to control things like washing machines. In this project, you can make a model AND gate to show how the output depends on the settings of the two input connections.

AND gate	A ○—⊐ ○ C B ○—⊐	
Input A	Input B	Output C
OFF	OFF	OFF
OFF	ON	OFF
OFF	ON	OFF
ON	ON	ON

OR gate	A ○—⊐ ○ C B ○—⊐	
Input A	Input B	Output C
OFF	OFF	OFF
OFF	ON	ON
ON	OFF	ON
ON	ON	ON

On or off?
AND and OR gates both have two inputs (A and B) and one output connection (C). The tables show how the ON/OFF states of the inputs affect the ON/OFF state of the output. These tables are called "truth tables".

MAKE A LOGIC GATE

You will need: *felt-tipped pen, ruler, stiff card in 3 colours, scissors, stapler, pencil, red and green sticky circles.*

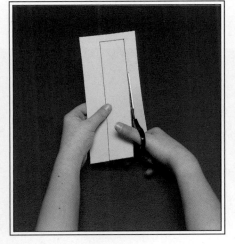

1 Mark and cut out three pieces of card. Referring to the colours shown here, the sizes are: dark blue 15 x 10cm, light blue 10 x 7cm and yellow 4 x 20cm.

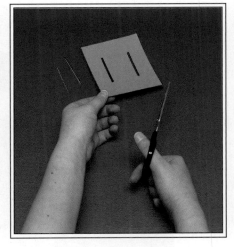

2 On the 10 x 7cm card, draw two slots that are slightly more than 4cm wide and 4cm apart. Cut each slot so that it is about 2 – 3mm wide.

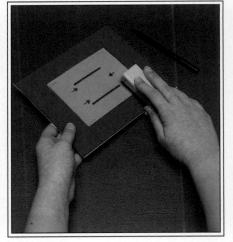

3 Place the card with slots in the centre of the dark blue card. Staple them together with one staple at each corner of the top card. Draw the three arrows as shown.

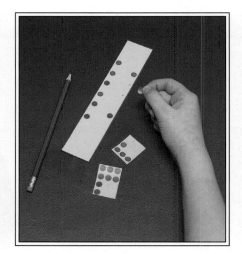

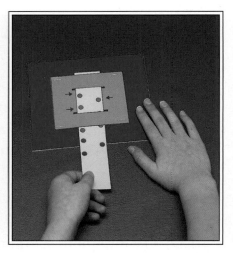

4 At 2cm intervals, stick coloured circles in the order shown on to the left side of the long card strip. This is the input side.

5 Add coloured stickers to the right (output side) at 4cm intervals in this order: green, red, red, red. Notice that each sticker is midway between the two on the left.

6 Push the strip between the two stapled cards and feed it through the lower slot. Keep pushing the strip and feed it through the top slot and out between the stapled cards.

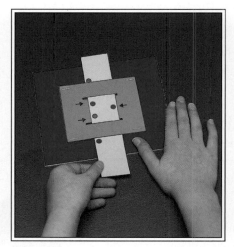

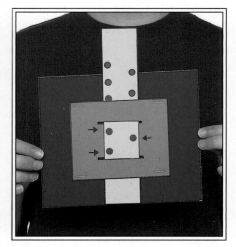

7 Move the strip until there is a green dot at the top of the input side. There should be a green dot on the output side, showing that both inputs must be ON for the output to be ON.

8 When the input shows red at the top with a green dot below, then a green dot appears on the output side. Your model is showing that the output is OFF when only one input is ON.

9 Here is your completed model AND gate. Now make a similar model with the stickers in the right places to show how an OR gate works. You will find that AND gates and OR gates are very different.

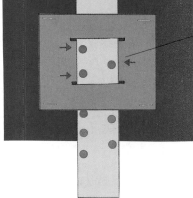

A completed AND model

Red dots indicate both inputs on model AND are OFF.

10 When both inputs on your model AND gate show red, then a red dot appears opposite the output. As you might expect, the output of an AND gate is OFF when both inputs are OFF.

THINGS TO COME

THE pace of invention has increased dramatically since the 1800s and there is no sign of it slowing down. Almost every week new inventions are announced. A recent invention for replanting trees by dropping saplings from the air could make forests grow again in many parts of the earth. Computerized map systems have been developed that make it impossible to get lost when travelling.

Many new inventions are things we hardly notice, such as the material Velcro which holds surfaces together and is used in place of buttons and zips on clothes. Some inventions are useful only in special situations. Kevlar is a recently invented, bullet-proof material that is very valuable for soldiers and policemen but little used in everyday life. Understanding of the genetic structures of living bodies is increasing all the time. In the future people may be able to choose what colour their baby's hair will be! One thing is certain. Whatever happens, people will not stop inventing.

Electronic circuits
Semiconductors are essential for making many of the electronic devices that we use every day, from pocket calculators to personal computers. Semiconductors are used to make electricity flow through tiny circuits in complex patterns that control how machines work.

Solar energy
People are trying increasingly to find new sources of energy because the old ones, such as coal and gas, will be used up in the future. Solar energy (the heat and light of the Sun) is one new energy source. This Russian space module, part of the international space station (ISS), is powered by the solar energy panels that fan out on either side of it. The panels convert heat and light into energy.

Russian space module

Village in orbit
The international space station is due to be completed in 2004. It is being built with the co-operation of 16 different countries throughout the world. They hope that having this permanent space station in orbit will allow scientists to make discoveries in space that will advance medicine, science and engineering.

Touchy-feely

Virtual reality is an invention that allows users wearing a headset and gloves to see and feel scenes which exist only on computer. Looking and touching in this way can be a very helpful way of training people to use machines. For example, pilots can be trained to fly a new aircraft without actually going into the air.

Talk to me

A scientist is looking at a graph that shows the word "baby" on a computer screen. It is part of research into how computers can reply to human voices. If people could talk to computers, using them would be easier.

Safe energy

The biggest problem with energy produced using nuclear fuel is the danger of radiation that can kill people. Some scientists recently believed that they had found a way to generate energy using the cold-fusion process shown here. The process creates energy by nuclear fusion without making radioactivity. It is uncertain whether this process can be used on a large scale or even repeated easily.

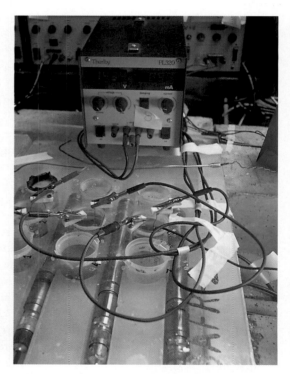

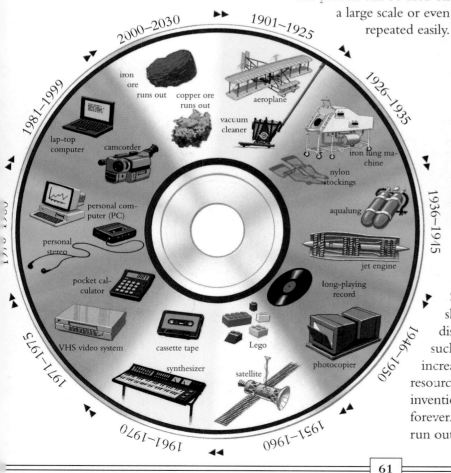

2000–2030
1901–1925
1981–1999
1926–1935

iron ore runs out
copper ore runs out
aeroplane
vacuum cleaner
lap-top computer
camcorder

iron lung machine
nylon stockings
personal computer (PC)
aqualung
personal stereo
jet engine
pocket calculator
long-playing record
VHS video system
cassette tape
Lego
synthesizer
satellite
photocopier

1936–1945
1971–1975
1961–1970
1951–1960
1946–1950

Still turning

Some of the many inventions since 1900 are shown inside the circle of this CD (compact disc). In the last 40 years electronic inventions, such as video and CD technology, have been used increasingly in homes everywhere. However, the resources on which people rely to make new inventions, such as copper and iron, will not last forever. In particular, copper ore will start to run out in 25 years' time.

GLOSSARY

acupuncture
An ancient form of Chinese medicine in which special needles are inserted into a patient's body to cure illness.

alcohol
A liquid made by allowing tiny micro-organisms to act on sugar.

artificial
Not achieved by natural means.

astrology
The belief that human lives are affected by the ways in which the planets and stars behave.

banner
Any flag-like design that represents a person's or a country's importance.

bifocal
Having two points of focus.

biologist
A scientist who investigates the ways in which living things grow and how they are made.

brewing
Using the changes that occur when yeast or other microbes feed on sugary solutions and give out substances such as alcohol.

carbon dioxide
A naturally-occurring gas present every-where in the air people breathe.

cellular
Things built out of single units joined together to make a whole.

chemical
A pure substance present in the Earth that can be formed by or react to other substances.

cholera
A dangerous illness caused by drinking water that is polluted with human waste.

cotton
Cloth woven from the soft material produced by the cotton plant.

data
Any collection of information that is collected for the purpose of putting it into a pattern.

disinfectant
A substance that is used for cleaning.

draughtsman
A person who makes drawings for specific purposes such as building a new house.

drug
A substance used for fighting illness. Some drugs are poisonous if not taken under the care of a medically-qualified person.

electricity
The form of energy produced by the movement of electrons (charged particles) in atoms.

electron
A tiny part of an atom that has an electric charge.

fax
A document that can contain both words and pictures sent from one person to another along a tele phone line.

fax machine
A machine that can both send and receive words and pictures that have been changed into electrical messages.

fermenting
The use of micro-organisms to produce the slow breaking down of natural substances.

fleece
The coat hair of animals such as sheep and goats that is spun into yarn and woven into cloth.

fungus
A kind of plant that includes mushrooms, toadstools and mould.

germ
A kind of micro-organism that, once it is inside the human body, can cause illness.

hertz
The name for the frequency of an electromagnetic wave.

infection
An attack on the cells in the body by germs that causes people to fall ill.

inventor
A person who finds a new way to make human knowledge useful in people's everyday lives.

keystone
The central stone in the arch of a bridge or curved part of a building.

laboratory
The workroom of a scientist where new ideas are carried out in the form of experiments.

lens
A curved piece of glass that, when people look through it, makes objects look bigger.